Contents

Our solar system 2
Mercury 4
Venus 6
Earth 8
Mars 10
Jupiter 12
Saturn 14
Uranus 16
Neptune 18
Pluto 20
Our moon 22
Index 24

Our solar system

We live on a planet called Earth. Earth is one of nine planets that travel around the sun.

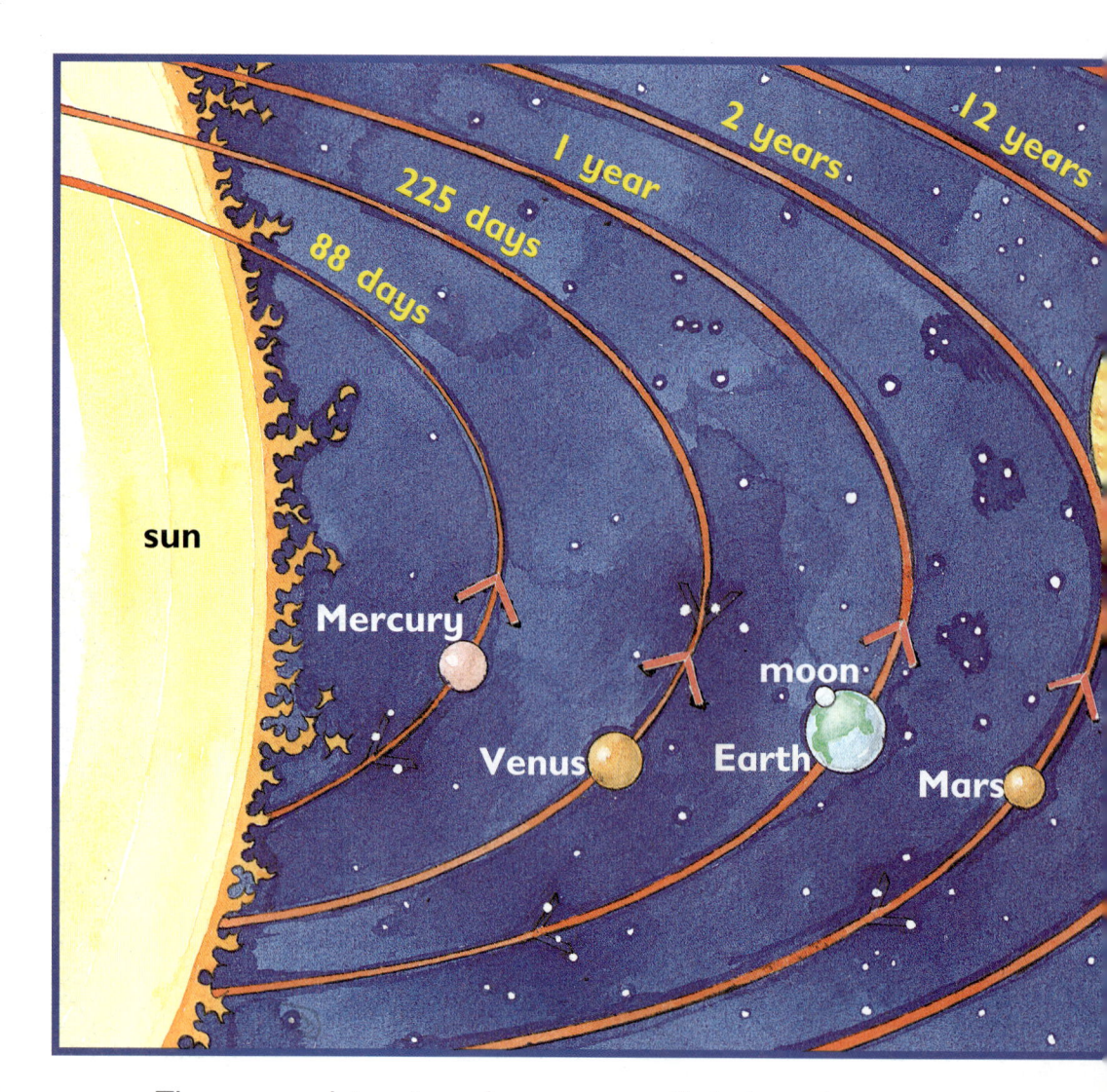

The sun and its nine planets are called the solar system.

The planets in our solar system travel around the sun in a circle. The circle that a planet makes around the sun is called its orbit.

Here you can see the times it takes the planets to orbit the sun.

Mercury

The nearest planet to the sun is Mercury. Mercury is a very small planet. It travels around the sun quite fast. It makes one orbit of the sun every eighty-eight days. You can see this orbit on pages 2 and 3.

Mercury makes one orbit of the sun every eighty-eight days.

It is very hot on Mercury because it is so near the sun.
The side of the planet which is nearest the sun is very, *very* hot.
It is so hot, it would melt metal!

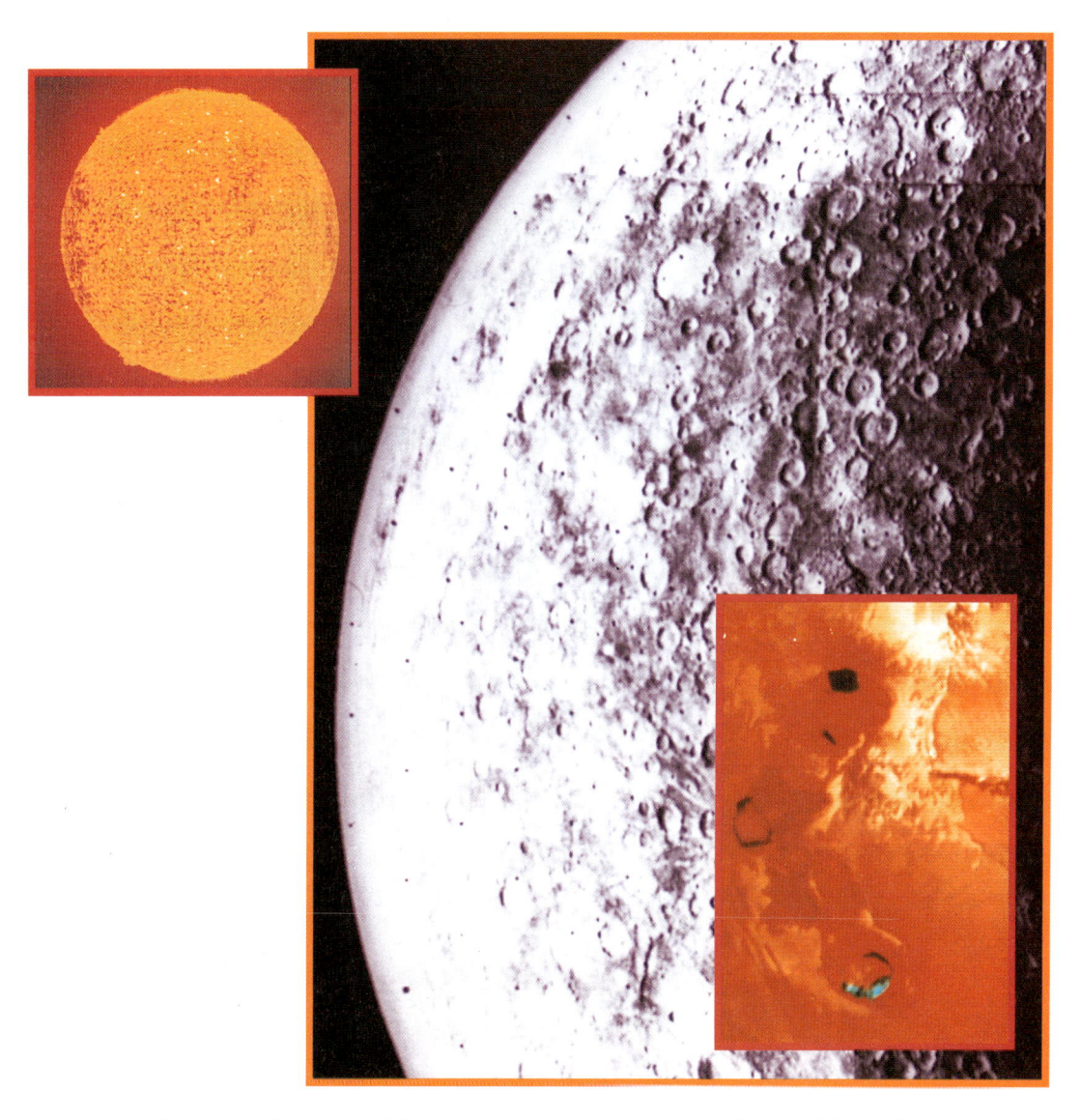

It is so hot on Mercury that even metal would melt.

5

Venus

The second planet from the sun is Venus. Venus is very bright in the sky. In the evening and at night it is called the Evening Star. It can sometimes be seen in the day, as well. Then it is called the Morning Star.

It is easy to see Venus from Earth because it is so bright.

Venus is about the same size as Earth but no one could live on Venus. It is a very hot planet that is covered in thick clouds. The thick clouds are acid clouds.

There are thick acid clouds on Venus.

Earth

Earth is the third planet from the sun. It takes just over a year for Earth to orbit the sun. That is just over three hundred and sixty-five days!

Earth is the third planet from the sun.

People can live on Earth because it is never too hot or too cold. Earth is covered in lots of water and there is air for us to breathe. These things make Earth a good place to live. Plants, animals and people can live on Earth.

People can live on Earth because it has all the things we need.

Mars

The next planet away from the sun is Mars. Mars is called the Red Planet because it is covered in red dust. It is a very cold planet.

Mars is called the Red Planet because of its red dust.

We know quite a lot about Mars because space probes have been sent there. You can find out more about Mars if you read *A Trip to Mars*, Jumpstart 3B, Book 4. See how many facts you can find out about Mars.

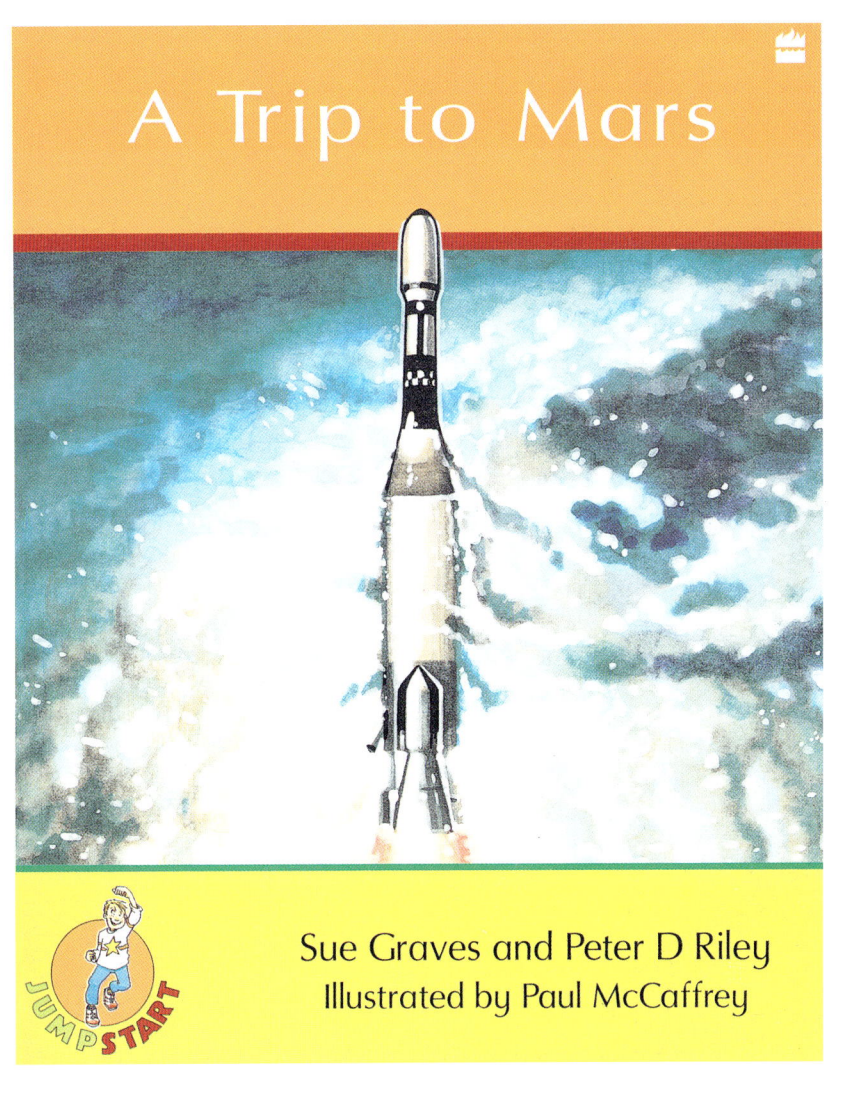

This book will tell you lots of things about Mars.

Jupiter

Jupiter is the biggest planet in the solar system. It is a giant ball of gas. Jupiter has a big spot on it called the Great Red Spot. Some people think that the Great Red Spot is a giant storm. The Great Red Spot is bigger than Earth!

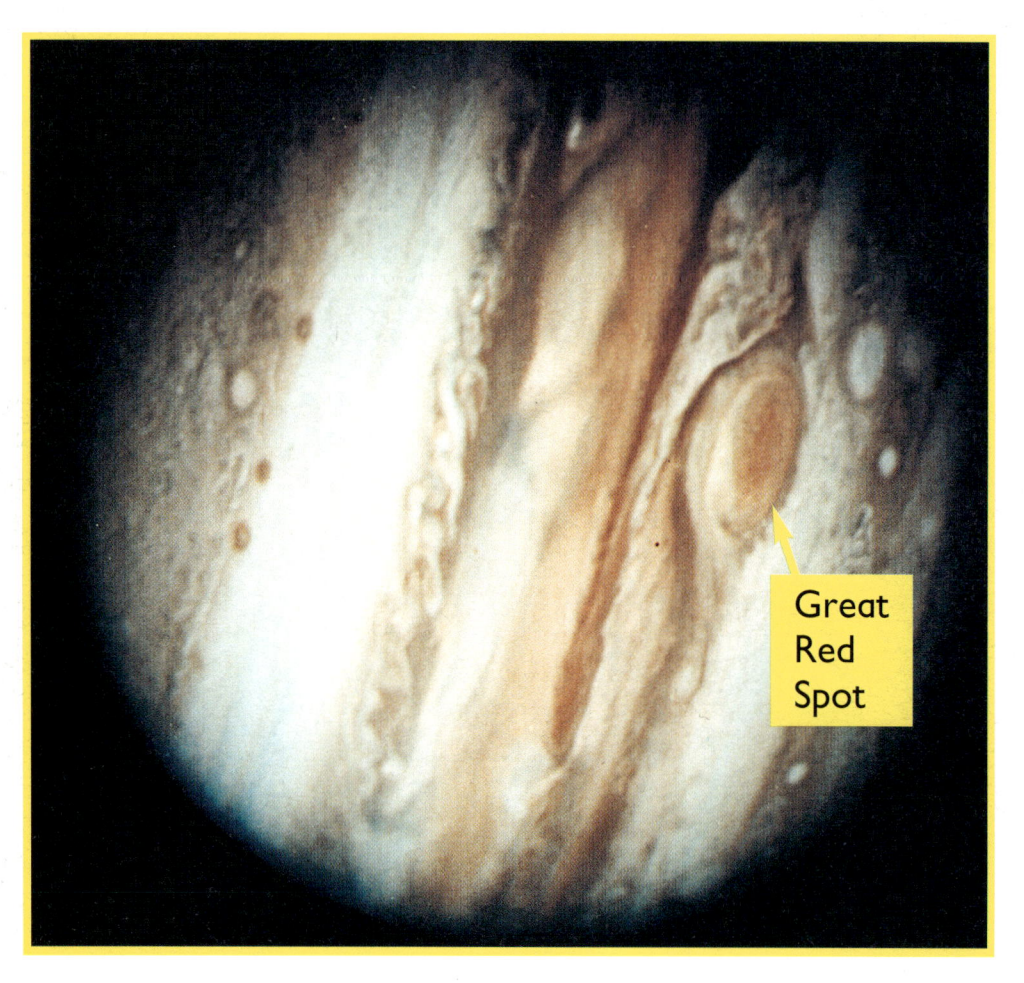

Great Red Spot

The Great Red Spot on Jupiter could be a giant storm.

Jupiter takes a long time to make one orbit of the sun. It takes twelve years to orbit the sun. A day on Jupiter is very short. There are only ten hours in a Jupiter day!

Jupiter takes twelve years to circle the sun.

Saturn

Saturn is a very bright planet. It is very big, too. It is the second biggest planet. It has seven big rings and lots of small rings around it. These rings are made of very small pieces of ice.

The seven rings around Saturn are made of pieces of ice.

Saturn takes longer than Jupiter to orbit the sun. It takes thirty years to make an orbit. Like Jupiter, Saturn has a very short day.

It takes thirty years for Saturn to make one orbit of the sun.

Uranus

Uranus is a long way from the sun. It is a big planet. It is a much bigger planet than Earth. Uranus takes a very long time to orbit the sun. It takes eighty-four years. Can you see the orbit of Uranus on pages 2 and 3?

The planet Uranus takes eighty-four years to orbit the sun.

Uranus is a ball of gas like Jupiter. It is covered in blue-green clouds. Uranus also has rings around it. Like Saturn, these rings may be made of pieces of ice.

Uranus is covered in blue-green clouds of gas.

Neptune

Neptune is a very big planet. It is four times bigger than Earth. Neptune takes a very long time to orbit the sun. In fact, it takes a hundred and sixty-five years to make just one orbit.

Neptune takes a hundred and sixty-five years to orbit the sun.

Neptune is a giant ball of gas like Jupiter and Uranus. Also like Jupiter, Neptune has a big spot on it. It is called the Great Dark Spot. The Great Dark Spot is a giant storm cloud. It is the same size as Earth!

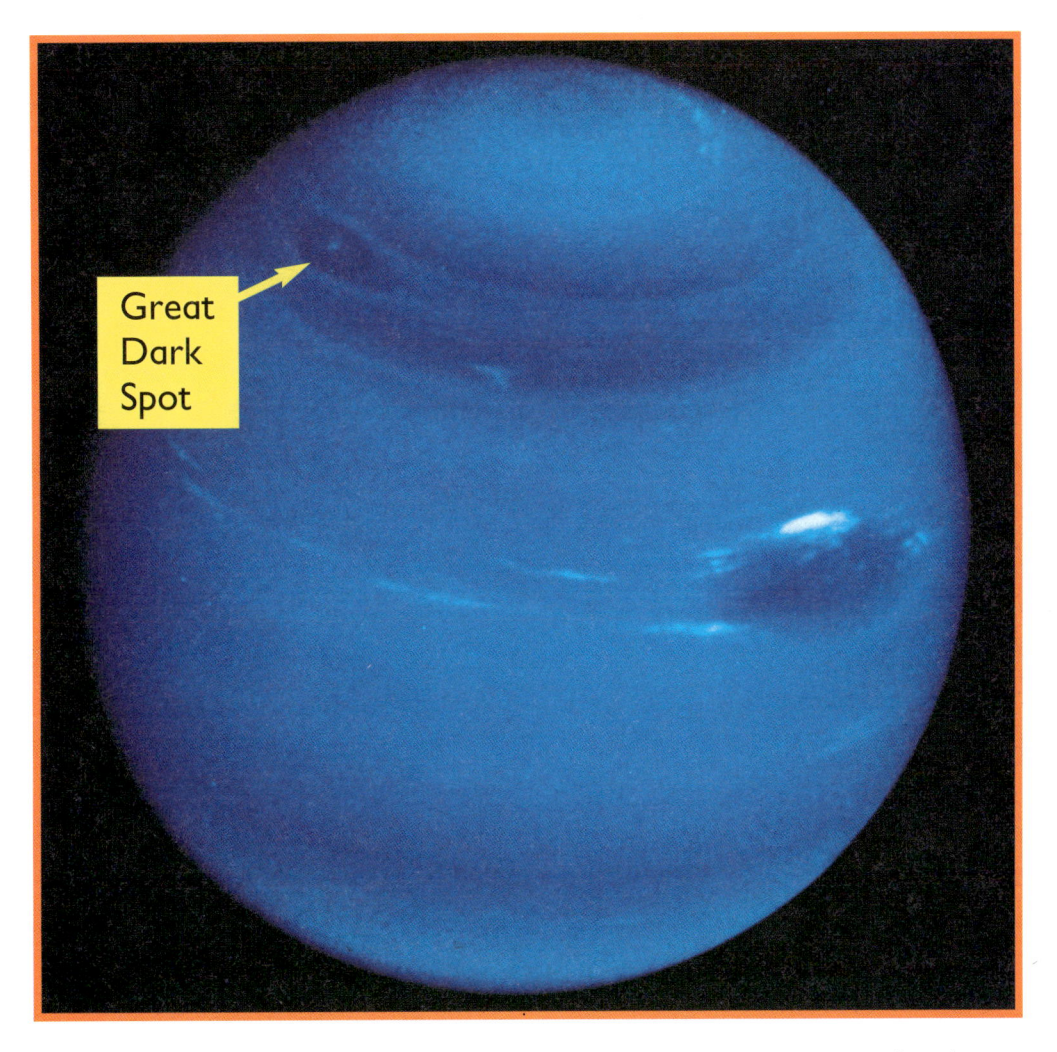

Great Dark Spot

The Great Dark Spot on Neptune is a giant storm cloud the same size as Earth!

Pluto

Pluto takes the longest time of all the planets to orbit the sun. Look at pages 2 and 3 to see how many years Pluto takes to orbit the sun.

Pluto takes the longest time of all the planets to orbit the sun.

Pluto is a very small planet. It is the smallest planet in our solar system. Pluto is very cold, too. It is cold because it is a very long way from the sun. Pluto is not a ball of gas like some of the planets. It is a ball of rock and ice.

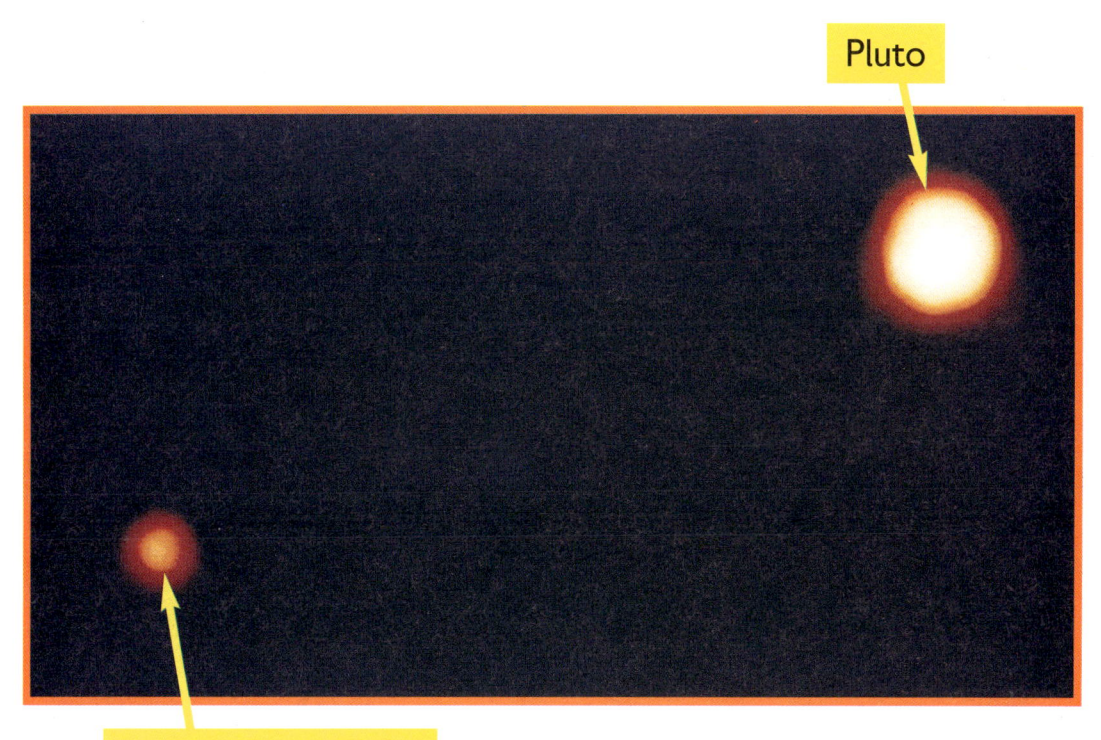

Pluto

This moon moves around Pluto.

Pluto is the smallest planet in our solar system.

Our moon

Our moon moves around our planet Earth. It is the only place in our solar system where people have landed. The moon is very dry and it is covered in dust. It is covered in craters, too. These craters can be seen from Earth.

The moon has craters which can be seen from Earth.

Did you know that the moon has no light of its own? The moon shines because it reflects light from the sun! You can find out more about the moon on the Internet. Look on this website: **http://spacescience.nasa.gov**

The moon shines because it reflects light from the sun.

Index

C
clouds 7, 17
craters 22

D
day 6, 13, 15
dust 10, 22

E
Earth 2, 6, 7, 8, 9, 12, 16, 18, 19, 22

G
gas 12, 17, 19, 21

I
ice 14, 17, 21

O
orbit 3, 4, 8, 13, 15, 16, 18, 20

R
rings 14, 17

S
solar system 2, 3, 12, 21, 22
Star 6
sun 2, 3, 4, 5, 6, 8, 10, 13, 15, 16, 18, 19, 20, 21, 23